THE FIELD OF INFINITE POSSIBILITIES

CLAC

SWEET AND LOW
INDEFINITE SINGULAR

the trouble with bartleby print//document

SWEET AND LOW :: INDEFINITE SINGULAR

ISBN # 978-1-946031-85-3
Library of Congress Cataloguing-in-Publication # 2020933064
copyright © 2016-20 by ELÆ [Lynne DeSilva-Johnson]

This text was set in Martina, Brandon Grotesque, Minion Pro, Arnhem, Franchise, and OCR-A Standard.

THANK YOU TO THE KIN THAT MADE ME FEEL I COULD.
YOU KNOW WHO YOU ARE.

THE TROUBLE WITH BARTLEBY
is an original artist book imprint

in collaboration with

the operating system / kin(d)* texts & projects
www.theoperatingsystem.org
operator@theoperatingsystem.org

SWEET AND LOW

LOW

INDEFINITE SINGULAR

work in this volume previously appeared in:

The Philadelphia Supplement
The CDC Poetry Project
Lament for the Dead
Big Echo

and was refined in performance
on many supportive stages

"In memory of feasible grace"
was originally published as a Panthalassa Pamphlet
by Tea & Tattered Pages Press in 2017

for you

San Precario
pray for us

There is no way out of a spiritual battle
There is no way you can avoid taking sides
There is no way you can not have a poetics
no matter what you do: plumber, baker, teacher

you do it in the consciousness of making
or not making yr world
you have a poetics: you step into the world
like a suit of readymade clothes

or you etch in light
your firmament spills into the shape of your room
the shape of the poem, of yr body, of yr loves

A [person's] life is an allegory

Dig it

from Diane DiPrima, 'RANT'

○

○

○

○

○

ALL HUBRIS & OPPOSABLE THUMBS

"Truth is haunted. You never get to the naked, shining, transparent, perfect bit....Ideas aren't colorless and flavorless, they have a specific frequency, a specific smell, they have ways of being thought."

--Timothy Morton, from *Humankind:*
Solidarity with NonHuman People

There is no scratch left to start from
no discoveries, no 'empty' land
no away to throw the unwanted
No not self
no self
No thing, everything.
We are haunted, spectral,
thick with each other
with story, with lichens and mosses
fish, goats, and roses
with stone.
How un-kin-d to presume
these miles "ours," to remove critter
or mushroom, to force another
to see a border fantasy
and call it by this name, as though
this deadly game was made real
through papers and capitalization

ROUTINE TEST, # 23-2908

what if what's in the throat
cannot be found by scopes or scans
or can -- but won't respond to
allopathic soothing mechanisms
what if what lives there is
the rotted, tannic, ossifying crumbs
of corkage, of the fingers
down the throat and over the mouth
or around the tenuous corridor
that tells head it belongs to body

you who spends so much time
building, amplifying
handing out megaphones
mapping roads to and through language
yet pause, and pause, and pause
heightened security always
at glottal's gate, lest
the Destroyer slips past
and the straw courage of this house
all pine needles and matchsticks
falls into the gutter that always awaits
mold or brushfire

.

"what are you up to" they say, wanting a neat reply:
job things or love things or maybe, neatly wrapped, art things \
(nothing too serious)

you learn to dissasemble, to
translate //

neurotypicals, I read, want invitations, engagement
not an explanation of what you're doing but a smile and an offer to come
on and join, assurance that they are welcome. their question is actually
about themselves. // here's another place to consider oneself "outside,"
then: I want to be left alone to work and play. ah,"only child," they nod,
in explanation.

no one wants my real answer, no "I'm working on being a pantheon / on
materializing into flesh / the animals and gods I possess." // here, in this
place, even fluidity asks to be tagged.

"what's your name" and "what do you do" open out unto a beigescape
spectrum from boredom to acceptable titillation / so that the asker,
humming, can set the gears in motion: open up the spreadsheet and
enter you on a line, punch a number in your ear, and move on, "knowing"
you by the familiar tropes you pinged // job / city / sex / alma mater and
the clothes you wore today // on you like leprosy // chipping away at
communion / until you aren't sure if speech / will eventually erase you /
transmuting as it does upon arrival / to expectant eyes and ears
you are not a self-help guru they signed up for, there is no green arrow
here, no GO. / these are masses not-inviting metamorphosis / but
confirmation, a version of what you were before you spoke;

A THREAT, A WEAKNESS, A WOMAN, A COLOR, A HAIRCUT.

the way you hold your body makes people think you have money because
it's the only commodity the capitalist body understands as power-giving
// the mourning doves on the fire escape pretend to be owls, reminding
me how to survive, who my friends are.

UP LONG ENOUGH

to break a glass
with a careless gesture
to undercook the white
of a 7-minute egg,
again.

even the fifteen pound blanket
is not enough to weigh
your body down
the parasympathetic nervous
system version
of clenched teeth - although
my actual face learned masks
in vigilance years ago.

it's a lie,
what they tell you
your face doesn't stick
like that, in the pleasure
of ugly joy, eyes crossed
and tongue lolling --
your body does
down to the hand it grows
in your neck
an adaptation
to remind you:

your silence keeps you alive
even as it strangles

i wonder if rumi was lonely, rilke / if perhaps loneliness is the purview of the poet / of the human with a prediliction for detached observation // can a poet of the people still truly be "of", be "alike" that / which one starts to see clearly? / isn't clarity immediately a putting of distance between?

(A)EVOLUTION FIELDNOTES :: ADAPTATION : CLIMATE [COLD]
entry: december 27, 2017
40.7829° N, 73.9654° W

Warm-blooded animals, which are mostly birds and mammals, need to maintain a relatively constant body temperature or they suffer dire consequences. It doesn't matter what the outside temperature is—they must maintain the same internal temperature.

20 degrees fahrenheit with a windchill bite but a bright clear sun that comes through the trees in this expanse excused from the cold grey shadow of buildings and it's like I've never walked in Central Park before: a seemingly foolhardy decision reserved for children, those at the behest of their still-euphoric wonderment-in-all-things, and European tourists.

Who do cold days belong to?

Never in my life have I owned cold days, I think.
Can I put this cold in my pocket, and hold it? Can this day belong to me?

Cold Days are the purview of the mysterious people who own things like snowshoes, by choice, because they can. Who own smart garments made from technologically superior fabrics emblazoned with Patagonia, North Face, Canada Goose. Who vacation in chilled cities, alternating selfie-punctuated walks with stops at Starbucks for fuel and warmth. Who ski, who winter-run, who are cold by choice, because they call its beginning and end.

Or, perhaps, there are also those who escaped scurrying's spell somehow, despite cold wearing them and not the other way around.

Not only do I feel for the pigeon, the rat, the urban mammal, I am this. I am this gray-thing, shimmering shape, I am ugly only with your eyes, I am resilience embodied. I am that which seems to have no spine when I need to squeeze this frame through tight places.

I have barely any shoulders. My neck is long for sticking out as needed. Just as they cannot help but be born in this place, call it home, eke out its food sources and seek out its warm corners -- only to be shunned and hunted on their doorstep--so too is this my contested terroir, and this level of play says: *Your resources are meagre. Conserve however you are able. Go out in the cold only when necessary. It will increase your hunger, your need.*

Disruptive events play out in the mind of the animal when triggered. Parrots, returned to the wild, have PTSD. I know I can only have a dollop of Maple Syrup with my breakfast. She calls it "Liquid Gold," and I must pour it very carefully. My hand shakes. I should not be trusted with things of great value. It will be my fault if we don't have enough.

We eat breakfast by the oven with the door open, in multiple sweaters and hats. The warmest square feet in the apartment. I imagine myself on ski-lodge vacations eating magazine pictures of drenched pancake piles.

In most instances, the size and shape of an organism dictate whether it will be warm-blooded or cold-blooded. Think about some large animals—elephants, whales, and walruses. Their volume is so large that relying on the outside environment to heat them up would be inefficient and would slow their response times, putting their survival at risk. For that reason, nearly all large animals are warm-blooded.

Who chooses cold when cold comes for you, caressing your winter nights with dead clam fingers through leaky windows and in the absence of warmth, landlords hoarding the heat like the pile of coins it becomes through their colorless eyes. The animal doesn't expose itself to cold. The animal waits. The animal has a plan.

When I was in kindergarten, we had an assignment to draw ourselves doing our favorite activity. I wrote "skiing," and drew myself on a slope, though I'd never been. When I was in highschool I hid my favorite, verboten clothes in my locker and added creative flourishes to stories about my lifestyle that no one could fact-check. Later, I got to choose my camera angles, and put my face and cherry-picked accomplishments on the internet.

These are the same fantasy, the same thing. Conjectured real, in anticipation of adaptation.

Did everybody think long underwear was for the weak when they were young? That somehow, to protect yourself from the frigid winds was something to avoid at all costs, wearing instead a hologram of nonchalance?

I decide: *my body, this cold, this ski-less life is not for me.* I counter my sexdrive with novena and pray to the gods that shake me to tears but whose rules, mistranslated, I bend to say the least. I say I do not feel the cold but it is my body I don't feel. I put it on a high shelf for many years until rust sets in. I burrow.

Often associated with low temperatures, the function of hibernation is to conserve energy when sufficient food is unavailable. To achieve this energy saving, an endotherm decreases its metabolic rate, which then decreases body temperature.

"Fooling Mother Nature: Forcing Bulbs for Indoor Bloom" explains that Geophytes (true bulbs, corms, tubers, tuberous roots, and rhizomes) have an extraordinary self-contained food storage tissue that nourishes the plant no matter the environmental conditions, be it cold or hot. I am storing tissue. I am squirrelling away.

The hemolytic condition occurs when there is an incompatibility between the blood types of the mother and the fetus. There is also potential incompatibility if the mother is Rh negative and the father is positive. When any incompatibility is detected, the mother often receives an injection at 28 weeks gestation and at birth to avoid the development of antibodies toward the fetus. These terms do not indicate which specific antigen-antibody incompatibility is implicated. The disorder in the fetus due to Rh D incompatibility is known as erythroblastosis fetalis.

When I am in the womb I kick and pound. My mother says I was hanging paintings, hammering. Me and Athena, I think. Her blood type is the opposite of mine. I require the serum of a Rhesus monkey to not become septic. This early incompatibility is known in literature as foreshadowing.

Difficulty breathing is common.

For years, the air is very thin, in all temperatures, so that I can barely find it.

December, 2017: It is nearing my fortieth year and I have come around to long underwear. I leave therapy and walk in the park, no matter the weather. I wear two coats under which I am nearly obscured, a large fake fur hat, boots, jeans, and underneath, a men's plaid shirt buttoned up to the neck. This is a silence, of the loud variety I prefer. I am steeled, but not impervious. Today, I choose cold. Today, I put cold in my pocket.

There is a gallon of maple syrup waiting at home.

NOTES ON ADAPTATION LOG:

For over a decade I have been researching and writing on human evolution and the relationship of that evolution to our material and nonhuman environment (really, the evolution of human as holobiont -- understanding the symbiotic relationship of forms ordinarily described as discrete to indeed have much blurrier lines.) In particular, I am interested in the *continued* evolution of human experience, and the ways this interfaces with technology, trauma, creative practice, energy practice, and, perhaps, choice -- perhaps, the possibility that (a)evolution, or auto-evolution, might be a possibility horizontally within a lifespan, as opposed to across generations as normally understood. As I work through healing my own C-PTSD from trauma, I consider the epigenetic imprint I may be changing in my own "nurture" adaptations, as well as how that changes my child, etc. This piece is from a larger series addressing certain blocks in my own patterning I am working to shift. The below are links I've used for reference.

http://www.saburchill.com/ans02/chapters/chap035.html
https://www.washingtonpost.com/news/animalia/wp/2017/07/08/can-animals-suffer-from-ptsd/?utm_term=.39c0d6b82b1b
http://pubs.ext.vt.edu/content/dam/pubs_ext_vt_edu/HORT/HORT-76/HORT-76-PDF.pdf
https://en.wikipedia.org/wiki/Rh_blood_group_system#Hemolytic_disease_of_the_newborn

breathe in for a count of four

for a count of seven, don't hold your breath
but rather imagine it radiating from your lungs
to your organs, blood, skin, tissue, bones
each of these inhaling, in turn
grateful to be remembered

breathe out for a count of eight

now: hold, and feel breath's absence

repeat, relishing and replenishing

repeat

situate a safe distances from the screams / where the murmuration
of leaves and sparrows / is indistinguishable// ask the moon if she
will melt you / until vein and ventricle, water table, / stream are
a single system / water and blood a new word / yet undiscovered
and unspoken, / but ancient, predating the clouded logic / that
bred exclusion //

HUM, here, dematerializing / until the space between (things)/
offers up its secret densities / a precipice undetectable / by the
tools you were given // still, becoming nothing / the horsefly will
land on you / because you (aren't) / there is no (between)//
let her teach you, motionless / until the breeze meeting skin /
moves through rather than over,/ with invitation,
acknowledgement, and relief //

remember: others will cling to a solidity that is real / as it was real
to you once / and it cannot be with frustration that you try in
vain to disabuse them of this notion. // (conversation) may feel
impossible. where is the line between a desire for a seen soul and
ego's learned fear of invisibility? //

you never knew how weariness and joy could be so close

ELEGY FOR THE ALMOST GONE / TERMINATION CODON

Chemical Formula: [C,H,O]
Molecular Weight = 180.29 gm

<u>Hydrogen</u>   11.18 % H 99.92 % H_2O

<u>Carbon</u>   79.94 % C

<u>Oxygen</u>   8.87 % O

———   ———
100.00 %   99.92 % = TOTAL OXIDE

Empirical Formula: C12H20O
Environment: Fossilized tree resin which is insoluble in common organic solvents. Gives an aromatic odor when burned (Plastic imitations do not).
IMA Status: Not Approved
IMA Locality: Gdansk, Shores of the Baltic Sea, Poland. US: Arkansas, New Jersey.
Name from Arabic Origin: عَنْبَر From ('anbar, Middle "ambergris"), English aumbre, from Middle in turn Persian from Middle 'mbl French ambre,
(ambar, "ambergris"). Compare lamber, ambergris.
Displaced Old English eolhsand ("elksand").
Synonym: Bernstein; Resin; Succinite; Xyloretinite
- C10H17O Gladstone-Dale: CI meas= -0.445 (Poor) - where the CI = (1-KPDmeas/KC)
KPDmeas= 0.4909,KC= 0.3397 Ncalc = 1.36 - 1.39
Optical Data: Isotropic, n=1.54.
Electron Density: Bulk Density (Electron Density)=1.22 gm/cc note: Specific Gravity of Amber =1.10 gm/cc.
Fermion Index = 0.0088532573
Boson Index = 0.9911467427 PE
Amber= 0.15 barns/electron U=PE
Amber x rElectron Density= 0.18 barns/cc.
Radioactivity: GRapi = 0
(Gamma Ray American Petroleum Institute Units)
Amber is Not Radioactive

Just as low temperature can extend the period of time that DNA can survive, total isolation from oxygen when trapped in amber is highly protective. Despite problems concerning DNA from insects in amber, there can be no question about the excellent preservation of tissue ultrastructure -- including ribosomes, endoplasmic reticulum and mitochondria -- for tens of millions of years [SCIENCE; 215:1241-1242 (1982) and SCIENTIFIC AMERICAN; 274(4): 85-91 (1996)]. Tree sap (resin) contains sugars as well as alcohols & aldehydes (including terpenes), which are dehydrating & antibiotic as well as providing an air-tight seal to prevent further entry of oxygen. Myrrh is a mixture of resin, gum and essential oils from the Commiphora plant that was used by the ancient Egyptians for embalming (by pouring it into the cranial, chest, abdominal and pelvic cavities) and mummification (by soaking the wrapping bandages in it).

Biological tissues can be preserved through:

- Low Temperature
- Chemical Preservation
- Dehydration
- Isolation from Oxygen

hu-bris [human, 21st c]: *R&D for an amber farm in the not-distant future, maybe Northwest Florida, or, better: somewhere in the Rust Belt, somewhere desperate for new industry. A hypothesis, a chemical formula. Lost in our linearity, hearing the tick of a clock we invented. It turns out, presumed ancient DNA was shown to be the result of human contamination, dinosaur egg shown to be fungi. Start over. Lose seed funding. Take down the website.*

Four-oh-four; not found. the server could not find what was requested.

IN-SECT: from early 17th century (originally denoting any small cold-blooded creature with a segmented body): from Latin (animal) insectum 'segmented (animal)' (translating Greek *zōion entomon*), **from *insecare* 'cut up or into,' from *in-* 'into' + *secare* 'to cut.'**

secō secās secat secāmus secātis secant
secābam secābās secābat secābāmus secābātis secābant
secuī secuistī secuit secuimus secuistis secuērunt
secueram secuerās secuerat secuerāmus secuerātis secuerant
secābō secābis secābit secābimus secābitis secābunt
secuerō secueris secuerit secuerimus secueritis secuerint

secem secēs secet secēmus secētis secent secārem secārēs secāret
secārēmus secārētis secārent secuerim secueris secuerit secuerimus
secueritis secuerint
secuissem secuissēs secuisset secuissēmus secuissētis secuissent
secā secāte secātō secātō secātōte secantō

sectūrum esse: You're cut, fold your napkins and go home.

we label /// gradations of proximity to extinction
enter: the passive voice where collapse becomes clinical

least concern
near threatened
vulnerable
critically endangered
recently extinct
gone
gone
gone
gone
gone

[   ] —————————————————————-

maps rewritten to pleasure and profit
maps precede the territory
greetings from the frothy wraith!
greetings from masturbatory overcompensation!
greetings from envy!
greetings from goodbye

COMPLETE CODE REWRITE:
IMPROVED PERFORMANCE WITH AN EYE ON SMOOTH USER
INTERFACE AND EXPERIENCE

habitat loss
> see: destruction
> see: fragmentation
> see: degradation
>
> *receive $10 off your total when you certify and purchase any Certified Wildlife Habitat (TM) sign. Limited time offer. Turning your yard, balcony container garden, schoolyard, work landscape, or roadside green space into a Certified Wildlife Habitat(TM) is fun and easy!*

> a commodity appears at first sight an extremely obvious, trivial thing
> what is in fact a social relation between people assumes the fantastic
> form of a relation between things

> *Do you have an insect you would like to display in a cool and interesting fashion? Then, you might be interested in preserving it in resin. Work in a well ventilated area. Make an attempt not to get any on your hands. It is very hard to clean off. I'm aware that another Instructable has been posted on this but my way is simpler and appeals to those that don't have a table saw.*

Y/N: [run data] can you fetishize the dying you cannot count or name

1702 : Data deficient species : avoid classing species as data deficient when the absence of records may indicate low abundance: If the range of a taxon is suspected to be relatively circumscribed, if a considerable period of time has elapsed since the last record of the taxon, threatened status may well be justified

REPLY IF IT PLEASES YOU: ___will attend ___x___will not attend

> We regret to inform you __THE LEPIDOPTERA FAMILY___ is unable to perform.

> We will see ourselves out. We are unbound by your temporal inadequacies. We persist in palimpsest, dimensional timelines beyond your feeble imaginaries. To think how you awed at a single specimen, pinned with the most delicate of care under glass, a careful hand marking and naming—honorifics, royals and heroes—only to blind yourselves to our evaporation.

> *Linnaeus chose Papilio for the type genus, as papilio is Latin for "butterfly". For the specific epithets of the genus, Linnaeus applied the names of Greek figures to the swallowtails.*

The type species: Papilio machaon honored Machaon, one of the sons of Asclepius, mentioned in the Iliad.[3] Further, the species Papilio homerus is named after the Greek poet, Homer.

Even with your own you direct the gaze: the pedestal, the stage, the pinned honor. Ignore the man behind the curtain, child. Denature and name, *shhhhhhh* cartographic carnage.

Swallowtail butterflies
- *Graphium levassori*
- Apo Swallowtail (Graphium sandawanum)
- Queen Alexandra's birdwing (Ornithoptera alexandrae)
- Wallace's golden birdwing (Ornithoptera croesus)
- Southern tailed birdwing (Ornithoptera meridionalis)
- *Papilio aristophontes*
- Luzon peacock swallowtail (Papilio chikae)
- Homerus swallowtail (Papilio homerus)
- *Papilio moerneri*

Lycaenids
- Illidge's ant blue (Acrodipsas illidgei)
- Cloud copper (Aloeides nubilus)
- *Arawacus aethesa*
- *Joiceya praeclarus*
- *Nirodia belphegor*
- *Orachrysops niobe*
- Dickson's Copper (Oxychaeta dicksoni)
- Bathurst copper (Paralucia spinifera)
- Vogel's blue (Plebejus vogelii)
- Zullich's blue (Plebejus zullichi)
- *Poecilmitis rileyi*
- *Poecilmitis swanepoeli*
- Mesopotamian blue (Polyommatus dama)
- Piedmont anomalous blue (Polyommatus humedasae)
- Theresia's blue (Polyommatus theresiae)
- Fatma's blue (Pseudophilotes fatma)
- Wallengren's Copper (Trimenia wallengrenii)

Nymphalids
- Comoro friar (Amauris comorana)
- Atlas grayling (Arethusana aksouali)
- Biak dark crow (Euploea albicosta)
- Murphy's crow (Euploea caespes)
- Seychelles crow (Euploea mitra)
- Biak threespot crow (Euploea tripunctata)

- Karpathos grayling (Hipparchia christenseni)
- Ponza grayling (Hipparchia sbordonii)
- Hewitson's small tree-nymph (Ideopsis hewitsonii)
- Moroccan wall brown (Lasiommata meadewaldoi)
- Halicarnas brown (Maniola halicarnassus)
- Kuekenthal's yellow tiger (Parantica kuekenthali)
- Biak tiger (Parantica marcia)
- Milagros' tiger (Parantica milagros)
- Father Schoenig's chocolate (Parantica schoenigi)
- Bonthain tiger (Parantica sulewattan)
- Timor yellow tiger (Parantica timorica)
- Madeiran speckled wood (Pararge xiphia)
- *Pseudochazara amymone*
- *Pseudochazara euxina*
- Schneider's surprise (Tiradelphe schneideri)

Other Lepidoptera species
- Madeiran brimstone (Gonepteryx maderensis)
- Black grass-dart butterfly (Ocybadistes knightorum)
- Canary Islands Large White (Pieris cheiranthi)
- Fabulous green sphinx moth (Tinostoma smaragditis)

Or is there a long table, fixed with Latinate names,
on museum board, penned in a flourish:
>*So nice to make your acquaintance*
>*Tell me a little about yourself*
>*What brings you here today*

So happy to be here tonight, (Hey Mom!) it's me, *Hemiphlebia mirabilis,* commonly known as the ancient greenling. I'm a species of damselfly in the family Hemiphlebiidae. I'm very small with a long, metallic-green body and clear wings. I've lived for just about ever in south-eastern Australia, buuuut my natural swamp habitat is threatened by habitat loss. I'm the last in my family! the only living species of the genus *Hemiphlebia. Hemiphlebiidae* represent!

Over here we have the fabulous green sphinx moth or fabulous green sphinx of Kauai (Yes mahma *officially* "fabulous" but you can call me Tinostoma smaragditis) I'm a species of moth representing the family Sphingidae. What's good Hawaii!

OMG, Hemi— same. Habitat Loss?! me too, bae, me too.
I mean, humans, amirite?

FUTURE PERFECT sevavi sevaverim servatus sum servatus sim sevavisti sevaveris servatus es servatus sis sevavit sevaverit servatus est servatus sit sevavimus sevaverimus servati sumus servati simus sevavisti sevaveritis ser- vati estis servati sitis sevaverunt sevaverint servati sunt servati sint survivors guilt survivalist survivor runt survive and run

recognate, re-tongue; preserve in and around tenses yet undeclined
ambergris, aldehyde and myrrh drawing lay lines
seeking reparations, weave-time y
ou'll need tuning, need
calibration
try
becoming
try
a backwards death

the place where you are is called here and you must treat it as a powerful stranger[1]

adapted from "Lost" by David Wagoner

wə'THaoot,wə'THout/

Action cannot be delayed because time does not flow from the present to the future — as if we had to choose between scenarios, hoping for the best — but as if time flowed from what is coming ("l'avenir" as we say in French to differentiate it from "le future") to the present. Which is another way to consider the times in which we should live as "apocalyptic." Not in the sense of the catastrophic (although it might be that also), but in the sense of the revelation of things that are coming toward us. — Latour

between soil and cumulous an infinite road
ahorizon line, laughing
you can no longer learn to dwell here   *wuon, wunian, bauen*
in the way of a body that knows itself,   *to spare and preserve*
earth, and the ineffable   *being in the world*

until the maps resist erasure
instead of insisting upon it   *semiosis,*
until there is, again, place   the triadic process of
between destinations   determination
until the everything is returned
to the negative spaces   *śūnyatā, stong pa nyid, kuu*
masquerading as void   *gong-seong, qoyusun*

they flit-speed-flit past windows:
landscapes left to urination   *The Adopt-A-Highway program,*
to footfalls only when fuel   *which began in 1989, has been one*
is exhausted, to   *of the truly successful government-*
the procession of the condemned: *public partnerships of our time*
us, moving through?
or the quickened
receding of the invisible to the forgotten?

into the scripts of planners
scraping her surface like a uterus   *construction of the Interstate*
the river's feet in eighteen wheeler   *Highway system*
stirrups, splayed,   *was a thinly*
these hills torn asunder, to bleed like   *disguised public works program*
a mother, and just as silently   *designed to prevent a severe post-*
as needful service continues,   *war recession or worse*
days open and close
and there is breakfast on the table

enclosed in emptiness there is only
the beyond, and even there
in the vastness   *246.3 trillion vehicle miles travelled*
there is nothing to list, nothing
located using these search terms   *bad command or file name:*
as your tongue falls flat and playless
on ears that moved on yesterday   *abort, retry, fail?*

our fingers remember the ghost stories,
the fictions of the grounds' possible bodies   *The minimal prerequisite*
and how our own possess   *for harmonic resonance*
their seeds   *is some system that*
survived in guano, in amber, in ice   *when deflected from*
now melted, molten, buried.   *some rest state,*
                                                     or equilibrium condition,
                                       experiences a restoring force that
                            pushes it back toward that equilibrium state

the mind cannot hold
what the skin can barely recall —   *Also required is some kind of*
even a breath dares not   *inertia, or momentum term, that*
disturb this slim   *makes it overshoot the equilibrium*
glimmer, our birthright.   *point to and pass on through,*
                                            continuing on to a deflection of
                        equal magnitude in the opposite direction,
                              from which point the restoring force
                will accelerate the system back toward the equilibrium center again,
                      setting up for repeating back and forth oscillations
                                  that can continue indefinitely
                                             in the absence
                                              of frictional
                                                  losses.

96 FOX HILL ROAD

mid 17th century: from modern Latin suicida
/act of suicide,/
suicidium /person who commits suicide,/
from Latin sui /of oneself/ + caedere /kill./

If woken from sleep
I may bolt up straight
fight mode engaged,
guns blazing

I barely know myself at times;
in the end
I'm just an animal

I'm sure of that.
You know,
there's comfort in hiding
in the tall grasses.

It's easy to hide in plain sight
in a town like Edinburg
with its feet on either side
of the Great Sacandaga,
land of the waving grasses,
stage of forgetting and being forgotten -
a space of erasure.

Lake's 90 feet deep
at the Conklingsville Dam,
choking the rush of the river's fury;
water, too, is an animal.

Quaint waterfront dining and antiques
belie a sleeping torrent,

a long unrequited love
of flooding this place:
of cleansing
of reclaiming.

Men lose fathers in a place like this,
fathers and brothers and a sense of who
and what it means to be
from nowhere in particular
paving so as to say
this is place,
knowing all the while.

Men settle alone amongst these ruins
in linoleum sided lions dens
behind the tall grasses
like moats, around.

Language is lost
away from mouths and hands
in this diorama,
this attempt at
an approximate life.

Where is sound?
Shots fired! Here is waking;
ammunition almost making you certain
of still possessing senses
making your way back through isolation's
cotton batting

the cold metal warm in your hand
sets mortality spinning present
your animal heightened to its
capacities and qualities

Desperation dials the phone
a last-ditch plea to translate

how the language of the shotgun
explodes the nothingness, if just
for a split second

But these uniforms speak gun different:
they cannot hear you
cannot see you
cannot know your hand's plea
your heart's breaking, spoken in shots
as their own animals rise
the discomfort of near death
filling their nostrils
not with a way out
as it does you
but with the snarled resentment
of a dog trained to fight
bred to be unfamilar with
frailty

The slight of gun-become-hand
that turns your gesture into a move
gauged offensive is
lost to rhetoric, to official reports
to ontologies of silence

to the somersaulted logic
of
"suicide by police."

DIS-/EASE CONTROL [CENTRAL]**

*dhē(i)- / dhayati, dhayah, thele, felare, femina, fecundus, daddjan

we are fetal, evidence of our vulnerable skins still
awaiting nourishment, awaiting permission to find ourselves here
to title ourselves <u>alive</u>

suckle, abundant, offspring, lamb

*terə- / turah, teirein, tornus, tiro, tirah, purh

En-title, I cross my self across my Self, transgender, trans species, I *give birth,* I *beget* my
Self, across, a diversity of bloodied letters

wounded, threshhold, to rub, rub away

*genə- / janati, janah, jatah, janman, gnasi, gentis, gecynd

to turn in different directions,
to bend
to turn aside

to raise, to lift, to hold suspended

these vowels   from- / their multiworld wombs
from- / the millioned mouths that said *wheel, befall, to be changed*

*wer- / aerein, svarr, schwer, vartate, rhatane, versus, weorthan, wyrd

Fecund filioque fellatio
I baste my wounds in eloquence, based in evidence,
the roots of my limb trees in *gignesthai,* in genius.
who I am but science-based, who I am but borne and born and bearer

Scilicet, sciolist, scission, scism, shiver, shyster, squire

*skei- / chindhi, a-sista-, skhizein, c'tim, chwydu

a stepping, I, permission. en-Titled. A fetus, I, the

secure ground from which operations proceed, the
destination of a runner

the *bottom of anything*

perceptible sight, a knowing
a Methodical Thing

tell me again how your hands came to hold
the title to story
how you knighted yourself use of my tongue

About this text:

The fascist impulse to control language usage is ultimately one of our most constant reminders of the power of language (things not powerful don't bear concern enough to control). These words are part of the ever shifting landscape of evolving sounds we employ to describe the wonder and confusion of our human lives -- and to mark these lives for ourselves, each other, and (we hope) our future generations, via story in all its forms. For this work I wanted to explore not only these words but also their origins -- looking for their overlaps across cultures and traditions, how they've woven in and out of each other, and already how this short list represents a galaxy of human history.

I wanted to speak to our enduring search for self, and indeed our entitlement to that search, and its journey through and across languages, landing us here, where someone tasked with our protection instead portends to tie us into knots. This is a poem of refusal and of grappling, that knows that we and these words are an interchangeable body, belonging to no one if not to all of us.

The text was created as part of the CDC Poetry Project, using words banned from the website by the current administration.

ELATED   SUPERNOVA   EULOGY   FOR   NEEDFUL   LONGING
REPLACED   BY   HORIZON   AND   LACK   THEREOF   (AN
AWARENESS   OF   THE   ILLUSION   OF   ITS   FIXITY)

feign joy in the last unicorn: feast

lay down your ploughshares
and have a heineken, together
lets talk about hops, instead
don't you love a good IPA
see, we can all get along
you both love hand pulled noodles
and compare instagram photos
of truffled kale chia bowls

yes, says the beer, let's be friends

and oh what a danger went there now
now you're like family, and
here comes "nice", good behavior
avoiding all the sensitive topics
so dinner doesn't grow tense

talk about food and other food
and food on tv that won best food
over other food, and whose food
was robbed, *oh my god totally*
and maybe about food you had together
that one time, stories of good times
you remember, of course you remember
reinforcing that *yes, yes, you are*
having a good time
here in this blank space

/what is the harm in it/
they say, /so you think we should
do penance, like,
and not go to brunch?/
they say, invisioning an alternative
of workhouse and gruel,
flavorless life and meals
spooned joyless from a troth

the density of our obsession
hits an apotheosis
where palate trumps character
and the entry codes to culture
are their own justification
their own reward
a tongue in which you must be conversant
to gain full access to the seemingly
unrelated arenas of critical
and personal
success

up close
no one loves a kind, smart person
with good ideas
working tirelessly for change
unless they can throw down
at the end of the day
unless they can show that
like stars, they're just like us
they go to the mall
they're in line at starbucks
they have a beer

A is for Allergies, Asthma, for "Alternative Healing," for unsolicited Advice (Again)

B is for Birthplan, and how it never works the way you planned, screaming for 12 hours in a hospital bed with a dural puncture, they clean the Baby Before they hand her to you, for tears in the Breastmilk, for Best Practices as a narrative trope, for the Body as token, as fetish, long silenced, choked, forgotten

C is for Cognitive Behavior Therapy, for CBD oil, for Canniboids, for C-PTSD, for Another Visit to the Cardiologist, for Cardi B's multimillion dollar Contract with Virgin Records and for the Creators carving a life out of nothing

D is for Daddies, for Vitamin D, for Do Not Resuscitate, for Damaged Goods

E, for Estrogen, for Esophogus, for Endometriosis, for Emergency C-Section

F is for Fuck This Shit, for Fear, for Feelings Had and Repressed

G is for Gods, All of Them, called when that fear Grips you, for Glottal and what is stuck there, for Gluten and Grains, for GTFO

H is for Hirsuite, for Hairy legs and the years of shame they carried, for Her and Hir and History Repeating Itself, for needing to be Held, for Holding

I (is for) the ticklish subject, erasure, for Isolation, Ire, for Isn't It Ironic, Don't You Think. (It Is.) For Isotope, Isotrope, Independence at what Cost.

J is for JK, except not. For Justice for All, ™., a slogan on a t-shirt, a Jukebox Jingle on tinny speakers over a minefield. Juicebox, Jihad, what Joy remains to be found

K is for the Killjoy, Feminist in the room, sorry not sorry, your joke isn't funny; for no longer Keeping your Kool when Kool isn't worth Keeping, for egregious systemic Kleptomania while the teenager stealing tampons from the drugstore has her photo plastered on Duane Reade's windows and doors. WANTED. Wanted: Kin and its building. For Kindness, despite this.

L: the first letter of the name the gave you. For Language that Leaves as much Left Behind, unspoken and unspeakable, as it grasps. For Laylines and Lollipops, for Lesbians who never had the chance, for Long Lines in time and on paper.

M is for Mother and all the things this isn't, mmmmm, automatically. For Media Saturation and Meditation and Mediation and Medication and Mud: being Made of, returning to, eating, Making pies of, in the face, My Name Is_____.

N: noxious, nothingness, no no no no no and no and #NOPE and C is for Consent I forgot to mention but don't you Fucking Forget It.

O is for little deaths never permitted. Oh, Oh, Oh, Oh YES oh YES; for Orientalism and Russian Orgies on Porn Hub and the way Organised Religion has left deep belief in the dust. Yet OH is my face and my mouth and my heart when wonder and awe Overtakes me. *Oh my god,* I say, *oh wow, oh,* and words escape me.

P is for Per, 1970's Proposed Pronoun for Person and how what I am called is not a Preference or a Pain in the Ass -- look me in the eye again when you say Pretty Pretty Princess, you Prick. For the Phallic Thrust, the Pretense of Product. For Phenomenology, and the Psychic Hotline; Perhaps the only knowing.

Yassssss Qween, let me tell you all the ways Queer isn't an *umbrella term* for the LGBTQ spectrum, isn't a style, a commodity -- Quit the obsequious show, the performative Quickening -- mourn and remember those who came before, tell it slant, don't quietly slip into straight lines for profit and acceptance. Query, Question, Imperative Tense: Queer is a verb, Queer is another, Queer is I do not accept your label, this system, these injustices. Queer the State, Queer your Family, Queer the Academy, Silence = Death. Quickly. Quickly now.

Remember the Body's Possibilities, R. Learn to Recognize Reactions for what they ARE. Recall, Reveal, Reprogram.

S is the Sneaking Silences that masquerade as Stillness, full of Sadness, Soaked in Sorrow. The Shallow waters of the Soul, So Sudden, Staking out a home in our days -- and the Sun, Stark and Sustaining, just as Spurious, here and then gone.

T is the Television on, my students cannot believe I haven't owned one for over Ten years. They draw a "living room" and there is a huge flat screen facing a couch. *How many living rooms do you Think look like This?* I ask. *Most*, they say, and Then There is quiet, as it sinks in. Trauma is here, too, always waiting to be acknowledged, if we are ready to name it. Take your Time, it says. I'm not going anywhere -- your cells are full of me, *my* program on, my broadcast streaming in the background. Trauma, in syndication. I too am in every room. Try to rearrange the furniture but I remain. I am the buzzing in your ears.

Utopian fantasies and speculative futures, You are Uranus, the planet swimming Upstream. An Upstart, Unsinkable, Untenable. United States of Total Terror we stand in fact divided and Unable to Believe our Eyes.

V and its Varied soft tissued monuments, V is *down there*, V is the doctors telling you your endo pain is Venereal disease, V is Veins on fire with flight, the Vagueries of the Vagus Nerve and its almost certain malfunction, this wanderer of the parasympathetic nervous system. The vigilance violence forces us to keep. The Versions of your life that might have been Viable. The Vagabond loses the trail.

Where, What, When, Why, the Double-You question that rips this World Width-Wise. Whirligig, the Wise multiplicities of Willpower and Water; whose Whole is this, whose Wreckage?

Another X-ray for the file, Excellent. Xerox copies of a former self, xenophobia not welcome here. X this box, X my box, sign below.

Y, Alice, you're back to You and its double. (Yes, And). Year after Year of this. Yellow was once Your Mother's Favorite Color, in her Youth. Yesterdays you've forgotten, Yesterday's News, Yabba Dabba Do You Feel This Way, Too?

Z: fickle object of so many nights' fruitless searching, Zoo the cruelty of cages from a species self-stripped of its home. Zenaida Dove, Zorilla, Zebu, Zebra, Zone-Tailed Pigeon. I Zig-Zag off the Z-axis with my animal friends, abandoning my tongue to ether, to Zero, to Zed.

The supermarket sign reads *"produces and fruits"* -- actions -- and I imagine that this place is very much alive, that it like I offers life unto the world anew, replete with bloody tissue, again and again. I read it on each passage, a prayer, this incidental street unusually strewn with detritus after the snow melts. It's wet, gray, and molty; the edges of cartons frayed and matted, into and indistinguishable from newspapers, cans continually too damp to rust.

The words don't go any farther than any of this, persistent and hungry not only without but regardless of my attention. I could fracture lines, but why. This morning I was unsatisfied with my rendering of the ranunculus, very satisfied with having done the drawing at all. 30 seconds, a few minutes. Reflecting the looking into a new mark. It didn't exist before.

You are magical, the world is a different one that it was before you made it — if not changed to gross perception. Accumulate marks and a record skip is possible *a record skip is possible   is possible   possible.* I have every desire to demonstrate that what I (know) is very little, but I am gathering practice to the body, learning from a list of mistakes that grows ever longer; perhaps together we can laugh at my foolishness.

A miracle of unfathomable proportion: we woke up today. That we exist at all. I'm super into the ineffable. My past lives keep me up at night. I don't mean to be a snob, I've just trained myself to be a catty asshole for leverage in this place. Call me on it. I can't remember trusting. My clothes come from places I cannot afford to go.

These are the words from the interstices, the monologue of stopping to listen, but objects in motion tend to stay in motion. I choose to continue moving, becoming more allowing of scales I cannot fathom, more compassionate to this body, more aware of the folly of fighting physics. Angle with and navigate sub and super lingual, sensory worlds, always in parallel with this surface accumulation, this hologram.

Parse and practice. Code switch. Sneak snippets of wild esoteria, spiritual anomaly, theories of time into conversation. A rough, crude go at holy, as evolution continues without retort and in ways unavailable, its edges shimmering. The system responds, pushes back; fissures appearing in the firmament.

Do you want to be a tiger? it asks, knowing that it is hawk that charts and soars through my days, at once precise and vast; exactly.

"Looked at from the perspective of the everyday world of appearances, the everywhere of the thinking ego—summoning into its presence whatever it pleases from any distance in time or space, which thought traverses with a velocity greater than light's—is a nowhere. And since this nowhere is by no means identical with the twofold nowhere from which we suddenly appear at birth and into which almost as suddenly we disappear in death, it might be conceived only as the Void. And the absolute void can be a limiting boundary concept; though not inconceivable, it is unthinkable. Obviously, if there is absolutely nothing, there can be nothing to think about. That we are in possession of these limiting boundary concepts enclosing our thought within (insurmountable) walls—and the notion of an absolute beginning or an absolute end is among them—does not tell us more than that we are indeed finite beings.

Man's finitude, irrevocably given by virtue of his own short time span set in an infinity of time stretching into both past and future, constitutes the infrastructure, as it were, of all mental activities: it manifests itself as the only reality of which thinking qua thinking is aware, when the thinking ego has withdrawn from the world of appearances and lost the sense of realness inherent in the sensus communis by which we orient ourselves in this world... The everywhere of thought is indeed a region of nowhere."

—Hannah Arendt

IN MEMORY OF FEASIBLE GRACE

[2017]

ESTHETOGENESIS

A process generating a reality in which all components, beside being the means to the self-revelation achievement, are also ends to themselves (the meaning of self-revelation). A final state of grace that only the mind can generate via evolution.

—Paolo Soleri

I am the Urban Mutant[1]
inextricable from this place
four generations before me
straphanging when there were straps
piecework and factory wages
in this teeming, seething anthill
where bodies exposed to high temperatures
become diamonds if they survive
visible only if you get far enough away

we are knit of the same fabric
its materials my materials
its pressures my native tongue

but the city too is not itself
was never a thing
and so you cannot be the city
even though you are
since you cannot be the city you cannot be

---

1 SOLERI SAYS that the New Yorker is of a different breed from the Iowa farmer not only culturally but genetically, especially once the breeding has gotten its own momentum. He warns of grave danger, of offspring whose goal might be movement to higher social and cultural niches, unaware that they are in the throes of the pressure of slow or rapid mutation processes governed by the iron rule of "natural" selection" where the "twist" is in the transformation and transforms of the natural by the doings of man.

just don't think too hard about it
and just keep moving

if you're lucky a trickster god
will get you a good deal on a place in Brooklyn
not far from train, bathroom in hall
cozy, good light
good credit only, no guarantors
nice girls only please ha ha just kidding
except not except we are serious except read between the lines
no one puts what's really happening on paper here

I OFTEN WONDER why we speak about evolution as though it were something that is over, of which a generous 'we' are the end result to be studied, a phenomenon in past tense. We watch the fabric of the globe erode and shift in response to our behaviors and materials, our stories, and speak of ourselves as though fixed objects. I go to the doctor and think about this.

I walk down the street wherever I am and think about this. When I am abroad I wonder what feels so different in the energy of the streets of Berlin versus New York and it's only when I return home that I realize what the lack of active bioprecarity feels like if you're sensitive to it. What I mean is: in New York City nearly every body is actively aware of its mortality, actively aware of how close its cells are to destruction. Part of its charm.

anyone with power learns that early
if your parents never had any
good luck with that, there's no distribution center
just figure out how you need to dress
what armor you need where
to pass unnoticed
taking furious notes

sometimes passing unnoticed
means your clothes will be loud;
these are not the same silences

survival is the hottest game in town

THE UNITED States is unique in its energetic tenor of bioprecarity—systemically breed- ing into its populace a genetic disposition for fear of an ability to care for oneself or ones family that is pervasive through most of our population, given the vast disparity between most US residents and the 1%. These issues are particularly prominent in our most vulnerable populations, with statistically higher occurrence in persons of color, immigrant communities, those whose families have been persecuted for their religious beliefs, those on the LGBTQ spectrum, and for the disabled and chronically ill. The longer one's family has been in this position, the more notable the consequences of epigenetic trauma on and in the body and the body of our children and our children's children.

every awning says original Ray's
yes the signs can just say "best pizza"
even though it isn't, you're catching on

surprisingly sometimes the best way
to camouflage oneself
is to stick with the herd

Uroplatus Gecko
Willow Ptarmigan
Toad
Common Baron Caterpillar
Tropidoderus Childrenii
Stone Flounder
Great Potoo
Katydid

I WONDER what to walk in the air full of this heady fear feels like for someone from a country where their cells aren't primed for danger. The electricity of a city like New York, touted as the purview of flashing lights and fast moving money, may indeed be most felt from its bodies in constant motion.

In American cities, surrounded by similarly traumatized bodies, away from the bioregulating processes and naturally occurring organic densities (i.e. forest, i.e. silences both visual and aural), competing for resources that are increasingly rare and out of reach, these stakes and their consequences are notably exacerbated.

in the insect world things are often not what they seem
especially if you're a hungry predator
For 250 million years, insects have survived
because they often appear to be something
other than what they really are.
Is it a bug, a twig, or a leaf?
Is that butterfly the bitter-tasting one,
or the delicious one that resembles it?

here, we are the Thracian girl, laughing
when we thought we would be the philosopher
but fuck, who wants to be down a well?

look at the stars alone in your room on your phone
so that no one sees you falter

AND YET, these things both are and aren't a product of the physical environment, which at times even in seeming service of the systems that cause these ills manage to stay their effects. Meaning — the physical plant isn't always in service of the system that exists with- in and on top of it. Just as the bodies aren't always in service of the system within and on top of us. Sometimes, what we've made can help our bodies hack our epigenetics.

Look up, look around. I have come to accept that much of the time I look like a tourist in my "own" city (the city that, according to Soleri, has become inextricably linked to my genetic makeup) because I do not cease to look up and around, noticing.

Lucky for me, I know how to do this without stopping short on the sidewalk. I am nothing if not a knowing conduit.

cry because they shine so brightly
whisper their names under your breath, or louder
if you can stand it

Eridani; Acamar; the ostrich, aulax, "the furrow," "End of River"
Cassiopeia ; Achird
Taurus; Ain; "eye", oculus bores
Lyra; Alathfar; "the talons of the swooping eagle"
Albaldah; Lucida Oppidi, "brightest of the town"

I WILL NEVER STOP being grateful for learning to draw early because it was here, in the city, pencil then pen then charcoal in hand I learned to see. I see the whole frame, its composition, major themes of light and dark at the same time that I see the cornice, its small architectures, that cat in the window, the refraction of the leaves on the sidewalk, the pattern on his socks, the way she cranes her neck to look behind her.

My students are in their first year of architecture school. I ask them how and if they think the physical environment of where they were raised influenced the characteristics they consider to be part of who they think they "are." We talk about whether we are from the city or the country and whether we were able to walk to get around, whether we could get to water or woods or town, whether we were isolated or amongst crowds, what colors and ages and religion and sexuality we saw and knew and became accustomed to not only with our minds and in story but in body.

They say they've never thought about this before and I say that's exactly why architects need to be reading and writing and listening and drawing and knowing the body and the world and the word, not just putting art as mausoleum for capital around equally blind citizens.

sing a song to Ursa Major, Arundhati, Alcor, Suhā; the "neglected one"
the shards of Arabic on your tongue, mispronounced
as unfamiliar as these galaxies
and yet as comforting

the city sits on top of the city which sits on top of the city which sits on top of the city
and it cannot ever not be a collision,
a sordid density where dream calls itself a power bottom
and sometimes it is
sometimes it actually enjoys it
sometimes amongst the shut eyed abandon
sometimes it remembers it-self-dream
sometimes my fallible body believes in love

SO YOU learn the body. And then you learn to look away from the body to know the body, back into the body, so that you look at the stars and down from the stars and still know your surroundings enough to not fall down the well.

And maybe you come to look at the city as natural, since the bodies in it are natural and our ability as humans to make and change and adapt and build is in those same genes as the end result of trauma. Maybe the same buildings and bodies that traumatize can be- come the site of discovery for their reconstruction. Maybe you can see Times Square again for the first time like the giant, flawed, canyon of yearning that it is and taste sweetness on every inch of concrete and steel, our infant species splaying its attempts at creation across our days in the most spectacular of failures.

NOTES ON LEGIBILITY, PRECARITY and SURVIVAL [2018]

I often find myself thinking about legibility -- specifically, how much influence an ability to blend / become / pass / be socially and culturally "understood" and "acceptable" has had on my life and work. It took me years to realize, however, that it was due to the level of precarity (financial, health and mental wellness, familial) and a recognition of myself as someone healing from longterm PTSD from various ongoing sources of trauma that my learned behavior became more and more performative, something I now consider a form of adaptive survival instinct.

Folks used to say to me that I was a chameleon, which I took with pride -- but what it meant was that I didn't see any entry to a transparent self in public venues; I'd never learned this was safe.

In certain ways (for instance, in my presentation as a queer non-binary person, a space I have emotionally and privately occupied since I was a child) the extent to which I negotiated this publicly (or not) might have been different were I 28, lets say, rather than 38. But, perhaps not: I would likely still have weighed whether or not I would be able to stay clothed, fed, and otherwise safe above all. I've never really been a joiner, so I didn't establish or find community to replace those safety nets I lacked elsewhere -- rather, negative self-patterning led me to other traumatic relationships that would echo the treatment I was used to.

But this isn't about me, alone. It's something I'm grappling with in my life and my poems as this process leads me to whatever safety I can find, and perhaps others will see themselves here.

The way I see it, the amount to which we are able to engage in conversation and read / be read (both verbally and also, non) in all areas of interaction can be seen to have a direct relationship to our capital holdings, and to our survival. This, in turn has a direct relationship to our assertion of (or obscuring / dissembling) our identity / public "self." In a culture where we're publicly trading these personas like playing cards, I often find we assume too quickly that one's publicly "chosen" or presented identity will necessarily reflect their inner life / experience. Transition out of a life of dissembling, especially for those juggling trauma, can feel like a impossible move.

We can observe how our ability to subvert this -- to escape, to choose an alternative to standard (or otherwise expected) tropes / scripts / patterns is (often) in immediate correspondence to / with the actual capital / security on which we may draw or rely. To be clear, I'm talking about capital as a dense concept, including but not limited to financial holdings.

Our relationship to these coded scripts has a wide spectrum of awareness / intention within which we operate. For instance, we may engage with certain aspects of our legibility (ie, fashion) with constant and careful attention, but even then rarely is this approached intentionally via the lens of strategic operation as understood vis-a-vis bio-survival / adaptation / evolutionary potential. However, many of us learn a code switching borne of a very primal space of survival.

Through Bessel Van Der Kolk's powerful text, "The Body Keeps The Score," I began to understand more fully that a *visceral* sense of "safety" (and, one including a socially reciprocal environment that is necessary in maintainting balance between the parasympathetic and sympathetic nervous system) would be needed to fully heal.

And here I land on whether or not this is fully possible -- and how many of us find ourselves here, in this bioprecarious space, in a system that feeds on fear, reinforcing it at every turn. I write and make every day in defiance of my reality, one which has left me in fight or flight now for well over a year. But I MUST. Maybe it will mean something to you, to any of you still living silent. ONWARD.

Greetings! Thank you for talking to yourself about your process today!
Can you introduce yourself, in a way that you would choose?

Recently I've been using a bio that says that I'm a "cluster of cells attempting to person," and that feels pretty right on. I go by the name Elæ, and my given name is Lynne Marie DeSilva-Johnson. There's actually a Catherine in there too. But I'm actively working in a space where the idea of a name is clearly troubled by a refusal to suggest I inhabit this word entirely, or that it encompasses "me" or my experience. I have a similar relationship to gender: a liminal, fluid continuum of possibility. Both/and. The name Elæ came from my investigation into nonbinary pronouns in romance languages, but I also love it because the glyph, like the use of they/them, requires a certain effort, an adaptive willingness to address and work alongside. It's only really entirely itself visually, and when you know what the word/glyph looks like, you know this when you hear it. And most aren't sure how to pronounce it. I've written, about this, that I want to be uncomfortable in your mouth.

Why are you a poet/writer/artist?

Oof, it's funny, I wrote this question and I rail against it immediately, but the railing is anticipated. Saying, "I'm not this" is as valid and expected, almost a more expected, response. It's almost a taunt. Right: so, I'd say, I will use the words "poet" or "writer" or "artist" when these terms gain me purchase into dialogues, spaces, resources, etc., that are inaccessible otherwise. So much of my work actually in part addresses the ways in which I think these terms, this naming, is reductive and harmful.

But I think what wants to be asked here is "why do you make things"? and if that's the question I would say this: I make things because I believe that I, and other people, need continuous re/orientation in order to survive and adapt and work against institutional programming. Marking, archiving, observing, analyzing, imagining, questioning, working through, and then the physical process of developing and honing material / tool skills are essential to personing,

---

1

These are questions I developed for the backmatter interview with OS collaborators that appears in the end of each print!:document. Here, I respond to my own questions.

what my cells are working to figure out. Sharing these makings with others perhaps inspires their personing, and then in dialogue we person / evolve together. Even when we only have our own self as audience, possibility and shift is planted simply in reflecting experience, perception, difference, speculation back at ourselves--especially when freedoms, selves, narratives are controlled, repressed, or otherwise dangerous to express.

When did you decide you were a poet/writer/artist (and/or: do you feel comfortable calling yourself a poet/writer/artist, what other titles or affiliations do you prefer/ feel are more accurate)?

I think I became comfortable using these terms pretty much exactly at the same time that I realized I didn't think they really held the capital that we're taught that they do, and about the same time that I realized I didn't need anyone else to grant me permission to do so. In terms of being an "artist," or "writer," who knows if I even am, or if any of us are more than all of us are, at least instinctively before it's broken out of us. I am lucky to have had a lot of exposure to creative making and lives growing up in New York City (I slept in Brooklyn but was raised by the East Village in the 1980's) and have had a lot of time to read and develop a relationship to materials. But I am mostly driven by questions, which is the best description of my medium / practice that I can give. It's an investigative, documentary drive, and within that a speculative drive. And I think I've always been that way, and done that. Truly I've always thought that's how we all are, and somehow I held on to the wonder. It's perhaps in part attributable to being a neurodiversity thing, but again...naming and how it reduces.

What's a "poet" (or "writer" or "artist") anyway? What do you see as your cultural and social role (in the literary / artistic / creative community and beyond)?

I love how Joseph Beuys talks about art as evolutionary necessity / possibility, in Public Dialogue, 1974...

> Here my idea is to declare that art is the only possibility for evolution, the only possibility to change the situation in the world. But then you have to enlarge the idea of art to include the whole creativity. And if you do that, it follows logically that every living being is an artist - an artist in the sense that he can develop his own capacity.

In thinking about this question I can't help but refer to a work that's been circling my mind for decades, which I frequently quote, and open this book with words from: Diane DiPrima's rant, wherein the "war against the imagination" is reiterated as "the only war that matters," practical, something people "die every day for the lack of" -- those who choose to play the role of "artist" or "writer" (and many who do but don't label themselves as such) have a massive responsibility / possibility of facilitating and amplifying access, and creating / activating tools for re/orientation and reprogramming via the senses-->body-->mind of a public both contemporaneous and future.

Talk about the process or instinct to move these poems (or your work in general) as independent entities into a body of work. How and why did this happen? Have you had this intention for a while? What encouraged and/or confounded this (or a book, in general) coming together? Was it a struggle?

Structure is my friend, and I work well on a project basis, or towards a discrete goal. This book began as a chapbook project I put together for a call, from work I had been developing primarily for and then in performance in a period of time when I was very ill. It had been a while since I had done a book project and, as a publisher / advocate of the book / publication as a tool for pedagogy and building one's practice I realized it was time for me to make one. It's evolved a few times, as has my practice, and this last version represents some changes made later in retrospect, now dealing with a work that is quite old. In order to insist upon the work being representative of me as practitioner and facilitator, it was important that it not only be a "collection," of "poems," but include other types of hybrid works, as well as some somatic / mindfulness materials.

Did you envision this collection as a collection or understand your process as writing or making specifically around a theme while the poems themselves were being written / the work was being made? How or how not?

The poems in the original chap definitely were all developed around illness and the body, and my experience navigating and thinking through not only precarity but bioprecarity, which I explain in the text at the end. However, I was working across a number of projects and individual pieces around and just after this time, and it felt right to me to cross-weave these other strands of my work / practice. I didn't think of the pieces as part of a cohesive whole as they were being made, but I certainly was aware of their linkages.

It bears noting, vis-a-vis the "struggle" question above, that the process of working with these two other presses (whose enthusiasm was also very positive for me, at one point, in each case) had whiplash upon the situations falling apart that was, twice, exhausting, destabilizing, and caused a deep disappointment in me which continues to have aftershocks. As someone who has chosen to dedicate so much time to amplifying the work of others in the community, putting out a book and taking time to even put one together was a long time coming and is a tender spot: I am a prolific maker, with tons of work I'd be happy to publish, but I'm only learning to prioritize that work being shown, published, and seen; however I was often feeling invisible, or rather, lost / rendered undifferentiated from the organization I ran and efforts for others. People will regularly approach me after my own readings asking how they get published with the OS. People I've known for years, despite me posting my own work and events regularly, will say, "oh, you (write/are an artist, etc)? I thought you were just an editor" which is definitely a deep groan-moment for me.

So, in a way, my choice not only to make the book initially but then to design and re-conceive of it and recognize that I needed to take a stand about systems of value and against gatekeeping in literature (so different in the artist's book) is part of the process too. It's not as much 'as the poems were written' but a continuous process of realizing and re-conceiving the book as a work, and what it could mean and be and demonstrate / celebrate / fight agains.

What formal structures or other constrictive practices (if any) do you use in the creation of your work? Have certain teachers or instructive environments, or readings/writings/work of other creative people informed the way you work/write?

Formal structures, constraints, and chance operations have become increasingly important to me conceptually, and in the way I think and engage in my creative practice, as well as how I teach (do in order to see in order to do). What this often means though is that I will determine the infrastructure and terms of a project, and follow it either to an end point or until pre-considered completion. I absolutely do use and encourage others to use constraint, found elements, counts, and other formal infrastructure, but often I feel like I am now inhabiting these practices, processing automatically and sometimes getting nothing "done" but experiencing and perceiving informed by these hacks.

It bears noting that I don't come from a creative writing background or any particularly formal training. I always wrote across various forms but by the end of college, I'd only ever taken one creative writing workshop, in HS. I had, however, worked in and for dramaturgy / writing for stage, as well found a lot of pleasure in scholarly writing across disciplines, and then using the forms and concepts from social science in my interdisciplinary practice. So the instructive environments for me were often those where I was taught to see, look, and hear, to use my senses critically, as well as to engage in research design, and then so too the stage and music: sound, cadence, and rhythmic structures, through many years of studying and performing across musical idioms and in particular jazz has had enormous influence on what now appears as my "written" work. But I'll often also say that text just happens to be one of my materials, and often one I can use when my resources are most meagre, and my body most challenged.

That said, when I later decided I wanted to explore what the "lit" world was even about, I began taking classes at the Poetry Project, and it was truly erica kaufman who broke down and put back together my concept of what it meant to be "inspired" vs. seeing as legitimate a practice that requires (indeed, demands) organization / strategy / administration. Talking to someone (erica) whose own practice was predicated on rigor and operation re-wired frustrations I had long been dealing with around some imposter mythology I was still carrying from the "muse" and "inspiration" type narratives we're so frequently fed; I think up until that point I shamed my project/process oriented inclinations, hoping I'd some day switch channels into a more romanticized "flashes of brilliance" sort of framework, which I think I was convinced was more pure or valid were it to happen apart from whatever projects or assignments I created for myself, rather than feeling excited about the flashes that were more adaptive or responsive to these sorts of frameworks I might design. Becoming aware of language and a sort of curatorial shift in validation towards Socially Engaged Art and/or what is now known as Social Practice art has been equally useful for helping me validate work that for many years in my early adult life I had little positive reinforcement around and was carrying a lot of trauma around leaving behind.

Work I've done with my students both in the classroom at Pratt as well as in workshop settings around constrictive practices and chance operations has been incredibly productive for me, it turns out, as have somatic techniques from across a range of disciplines; embodiment and physicalized engagement has been continuously central in my work for many years now.

Were I to begin listing the number of people or things that I could or should reference that have or continue to influence me, this book would never come out. It helps, though, that every day these shift, and also that I can with confidence say that the smallest things inspire and influence, as well as high-culture and/or scholarly/pedagogical sources. I'd be remiss here not to mention Buckminster Fuller, whose approach and theories continue to inspire, as well as Ursula K. LeGuin, and to that end many others who since my earliest memories have encouraged me to live and spend psychic time in a speculative space, rather than the linguistically / perceptually delimited frame we're often confined to in meattime. I'm constantly inspired by the work that comes in and through the OS. People are making and doing truly brilliant, innovative things.

Speaking of monikers, what does your title represent? How was it generated? Talk about the way you titled the book, and how your process of naming (individual pieces, sections, etc) influences you and/or colors your work specifically.

Funny, I don't entirely remember where *Sweet and Low* came from, though I can say confidently that the work emerged from a time in which I needed to rewrite my relationship to my body, and then to time and space and other bodies, in response. This brought me to some of my lowest points, but also to some of my sweetest, as I began to offer a sort of solace and care to parts of myself desperately in need of kindness.

In "Six Ways of Looking at Crip Time," Ellen Samuels writes that "crip time is time travel," bending the clock to the wont of the body outside an ableist framework of expectation. In works like this, in the years I (re-)acquainted myself with a new body with new needs, I found a permission, even a celebration, in what could be learned in these spaces which could be liberatory and sweeter than imagined. The "crip emotional intelligence," as Leah Lakshmi Piepzna-Samarasinha terms it, in *Care Work: Dreaming Disability Justice*, that I came to know in myself and in others I connected with through our bodies other-maps, provided new dictionaries for almost everything I knew and saw in myself and others. An experience, indeed, both *Sweet* and *Low*.

In this book's evolution, from an initial call prompt to an offer at publication at a small Canadian press (with no US distribution and no paperwork; I pulled it) to an offer of publication with a press I loved (which then closed a few months before release), I began to rework certain parts of it, until it felt sometimes like a golem, franken-book, unrecognizable, and yet something I still felt dedicated to releasing like a satellite. In this time, as I also released AFAB pronouns entirely and moved to an expansive liminal naming for myself, it felt right to allow this title to evolve, too: *indefinite singular* refers not only to the work's incessant lack of fixity but to my own. This phrase describes pronouns whose subjects cannot be pinned down: one, anyone, everyone, no one, someone, anybody, everybody, nobody, somebody, another, the other, either, neither, each, little, less, much, both, few, fewer, many, others, several, all, any, more, most, none, some, and so on. This book and I... are indefinite. I'm less sure on the singular, but we'll count this body as a [1], for the sake of the game.

What does this book DO (as much as what it says or contains)?

Oh, I love(d) (writing this) question (and giving it to people)! In its contents, it refuses to be bowed by formal convention, it explores modalities of scholarship and somatic / embodied possibility, it prays and enumerates and decries and gives witness to. But it also, I hope, says NO GATEKEEPERS and encourages you to fly that banner high. It is a critical kicking to the curb, for me, of whatever remnant of waiting for the validation of others was still worming its way into my gray matter. Rome is burning, there's no time for that insidious venom. BYE FELICIA.

What would be the best possible outcome for this book? What might it do in the world, and how will its presence as an object facilitate your creative role in your community and beyond? What are your hopes for this book, and for your practice?

I would like to see others, working with text, especially those who already have well respected books, publishing their own works on their own presses or independently, as artists do artist's books. I hope this inspires others to release granting others' permission to devalue them or their work. I believe book objects can serve as talisman and scrying stone into a potential future, carrying our words and work into worlds and minds beyond our own in ways beyond our imagining. These small seedlings have infinite possibilities I cannot possibly predict, but it is the planting I'm excited about, both for growth I experience and for that I may never know of, in others' universes.

Let's talk a little bit about the role of poetics and creative community in social and political activism, so present in our daily lives as we face the often sobering, sometimes dangerous realities of the Capitalocene. How does your process, practice, or work otherwise interface with these conditions?

I began this book with RANT, I began this interview with RANT, and here I go again, I'm thinking about RANT. But it's because again I want to return to the danger of a life devoid of questions, in which curiosity has been discouraged, in which disembodiment and disconnection from the natural world can often become a matter of survival within a hyperreal human framework that threatens to overwrite all other programs.

My practice, and the practice I hope to encourage in my students (no matter their discipline) is that of the question, is that of assessing and seeking to address the grave and wondrous conditions of our time, our species, and the vastness within which we are an infinitessimally minute speck.

There is a great deal of awe in my work, I hope, and I also hope to convey how much I know I don't know, and know I know I don't know. It seeks to find the thin bridge where an informed lover of language with a scholarly bent writes loving and somehow well-received invitations to roundtable dialogues about fear and possibility and trauma with kin and strangers, all the while honoring non-human allies.

I fear, at least in the US, that our institutions (and classrooms, part and parcel of) are largely lost to us as spaces that are connecting with the large portion of the population. But I believe that creative output, in simultaneously stimulating mind and sensory body, perhaps is the most unifying human experience / product, and thereby what falls under the umbrella of the 'arts,' may be best positioned to be the space of learning in this time of backlash and recovery from institutional atrophy. It's also where we're seeing the work of healing, scientific inquiry / citizen science, human-AI exploration, and countless other inquiries happening in spaces that aren't confined by the strangulation of institutional regulation.

Back to Beuys, then, here we evolve? All of us, artists, all of us with the purple crayon. We desperately need it. I hope to call for action by way of doing / making / asking, with humility and true desire for others to take up the mantle alongside, with no masters.

ONWARD, indeed.

ELÆ [Lynne DeSilva-Johnson] is a cell cluster attempting to person.

A nonbinary, gender expansive, queer AF splat of universe.

For legibility and fungibility: they are a multimodal creative practitioner, curator, cultural scholar and educator. Their work employs text, installation, sound design, performance, digital tech and speculative theory in addressing the somatic, ontological intersections between persons, forms of language, and systems, as well as the study of resilient, open source strategies for ecological and social change. Features include *How to Human: Resistance Protocols* as part of Performing Knowledge at the Segal Center, the *Speculative Resilience Radical*

Practice Library & Lab for the Anarchist Bookfair, Dixon Place's *HOT!* Festival, and a field lab installation for Ars Electronica / STWST. Publications include *Vestiges, Big Echo, Matters of Feminist Practice, The Transgender Narratives Anthology, Choice Words: Writers on Abortion,* and many more. Solo text projects include *Ground, Blood Altas, Overview Effect, Sweet and Low: Indefinite Singular,* and the collaborative *Boddy Oddy Oddy,* an ekphrastic project with painter Georgia Elrod, and *The Precarity Bodyhacking Work-Book and Guide,* with Cory Tamler and Storm Budwig. Hats: Visiting Assistant Professor at Pratt Institute, Founder/ Creative Director of The Operating System / Liminal Lab, Communications Manager for More Art, and lead R&D for the Brooklyn node of the Mycelium Network Society. A door via IG: @thetroublewithbartleby

about THE TROUBLE WITH BARTLEBY

THE TROUBLE WITH BARTLEBY is now an "imprint," which means a lot but also nothing. It means I can create digital papertrails, a certain DNA, in data connecting my projects' 0's and 1's, as I publish and distribute through online means. Analogue, it's also the name I gave to the "press" I began in producing two editioned artist chapbooks in 2012 for the CUNY Chapbook Festival in 2012, *Ground* and *Blood Atlas.*

Around this time, when, in conjunction with the magazine *Exit Strata,* I decided to lead a chapbook "charrette" modeled on design charrettes (helping others to break the psychic ceiling as I had done with making and selling my own book), we published these as Exit Strata books in collaboration with The Trouble With Bartleby, and to this day the last page of every Operating System book, a sort of DOC U MENT manifesto, reads, "the print! document series / is a project of / the trouble with bartleby / in collaboration with / the operating system." Which means, basically, that I am having a meta cluster fuck of performative-organizational identities, but that no matter what the roots are here, in *The Trouble With Bartleby,* understood as an experiment in value-adding, perception, re/orientation, resource distribution, agency reclamation, etc.

It's also the name I gave my blog starting way back in 2003, and has its origins in the line that had always stuck with me since my first, mid-1990's reading of Melville's "Bartleby the Scrivener," which is: "I would prefer not to."

That blog lived, with some fallow periods, from 2003 to 2016, and still exists in evergreen archival form at http://thetroublewithbartleby.net. Therein lives the original Poetry Month 30/30/30 that I tasked *myself* that would eventually grow into the OS's long-running series, now in its 9th year, amongst so much more.

In the section of the blog entitled "Bartleby at the Blackboard: Philosophy (Im)Practicum," it is explained (in third person), that:

> *As much as Bartleby prefers to keep a healthy distance from the Ideological State Apparati, we've nonetheless managed to create and maintain a relationship of mutual understanding with the English Department at the City College of New York, where Lynne DeSilva-Johnson has been teaching as an Adjunct Lecturer for six years and counting.*
>
> *She is hoping that per Melville that her refusal to fully vet or participate in these apparati will eventually lead to her being left to herself in the proverbial office, doing as she will. Nay, she intends very much for this to happen, in particular as the mortar loosens more and more (2012 FTW!)*

Elsewhere on the blog, somewhere late in its life I look back on its origins, in seeking a space of public, free-from-institutional-expectations-and-norms rigor for my writing, both "creative" and theoretical, which I've continued to seek for almost two decades.

The point of including this back story is that it is necessary to understand the throughline of what came later: the "print document" theories of the OS, the self-publishing experiments, the consideration of open source models for self and other, for pedagogy and extra-institutional learning, growth, and resource sharing, etc., as having its original roots in this blog, insofar as it represents my initial foray beyond institutional and/or legitimized top-down, "publishing," allowing direct production and immediate, globally scaled communications with both known and infinitely unknown audiences.

This would be followed by experiments in Citizen Journalism like Broowaha starting in the early 00's, predating Medium by many years. But it also coincided with being inspired in my research and projects by looking back and being inspired by individual humans and collectives deciding to not only talk about seizing the means but doing it and making it possible for others to do the same.

Could I hold space for myself? Could I hold space for others? Could I encourage others to hold space for *themselves*? I believed I could. It felt like life, in a way I had begun to worry might not be possible.

The point is, though, Bartleby and the OS and all related projects have always been a reflexive, public experiment, performed and always adapting, with no pretense of not being performance / experimentation.

The Trouble With Bartleby, like the human person whose work it represents, exists in liminal space, which is to say it both is there and isn't; a paradox. Expansive, nonbinary, like the gender of that person. It looks and smells like a press, or like an arts organization, but mostly it uses those words simply to *pass*—an operation familiar to so many folx in the QTGNC community that has always been so tightly connected to the OS, and to {me}/bartleby/elæ / ∞, etc. {language, though, amirite}

It feels, as I write this, in 2020, that the outgrowth began to lose track of its intentional codeswitch, allowing for too much blurring between the lines of performative publishing / engagement in the publishing industry and my / the OS's original, anarchic intentions around anti-institutional *training*, peer2peer resource sharing, scaled labor/barter systems. You'll find the original plan at Heroes and Hobos, a stillborn wordpress, but I had to come in the door through this Trojan Horse, playing at the validation models we at the same time, with every breath, refused to seek and actively spoke out against.

Today, I seek to reclaim those origins.

The Operating System uses the language "print document" to differentiate from the book-object as part of our mission to distinguish the act of documentation-in-book-FORM from the act of publishing as a backwards-facing replication of the book's agentive *role* as it may have appeared the last several centuries of its history. Ultimately, I approach the book as TECHNOLOGY: one of a variety of printed documents (in this case, bound) that humans have invented and in turn used to archive and disseminate ideas, beliefs, stories, and other evidence of production.

Ownership and use of printing presses and access to (or restriction of printed materials) has long been a site of struggle, related in many ways to revolutionary activity and the fight for civil rights and free speech all over the world. While (in many countries) the contemporary quotidian landscape has indeed drastically shifted in its access to platforms for sharing information and in the widespread ability to "publish" digitally, even with extremely limited resources, the importance of publication on physical media has not diminished. In fact, this may be the most critical time in recent history for activist groups, artists, and others to insist upon learning, establishing, and encouraging personal and community documentation practices. Hear me out.

With The OS's print endeavors I wanted to open up a conversation about this: the ultimately radical, transgressive act of creating PRINT /DOCUMENTATION in the digital age. It's a question of the archive, and of history: who gets to tell the story, and what evidence of our life, our behaviors, our experiences are we leaving behind? We can know little to nothing about the future into which we're leaving an unprecedentedly digital document trail — but we can be assured that publications, government agencies, museums, schools, and other institutional powers that be will continue to leave BOTH a digital and print version of their production for the official record. Will we?

As a (rogue) anthropologist and long time academic, I can easily pull up many accounts about how lives, behaviors, experiences — how THE STORY of a time or place — was pieced together using the deep study of correspondence, notebooks, and other physical documents which are no longer the norm in many lives and practices. As we move our creative behaviors towards digital note taking, and even audio and video, what can we predict about future technology that is in any way assuring that our stories will be accurately told – or told at all? How will we leave these things for the record?

In these documents we say:
WE WERE HERE, WE EXISTED, WE HAVE A DIFFERENT STORY

- Elæ [Lynne DeSilva-Johnson], Founder/Creative Director
THE OPERATING SYSTEM, Brooklyn NY 2020

DOC U MENT
/däkyəmənt/

First meant "instruction" or "evidence," whether written or not.

noun - a piece of written, printed, or electronic matter that provides information or evidence or that serves as an official record
verb - record (something) in written, photographic, or other form
synonyms - paper - deed - record - writing - act - instrument

[*Middle English, precept, from Old French, from Latin documentum, example, proof, from docre, to teach; see dek- in Indo-European roots.*]

Who is responsible for the manufacture of value?

Based on what supercilious ontology have we landed in a space where we vie against other creative people in vain pursuit of the fleeting credibilities of the scarcity economy, rather than freely collaborating and sharing openly with each other in ecstatic celebration of MAKING?

While we understand and acknowledge the economic pressures and fear-mongering that threatens to dominate and crush the creative impulse, we also believe that *now more than ever we have the tools to relinquish agency via cooperative means,* fueled by the fires of the Open Source Movement.

Looking out across the invisible vistas of that rhizomatic parallel country we can begin to see our community beyond constraints, in the place where intention meets resilient, proactive, collaborative organization.

Here is a document born of that belief, sown purely of imagination and will.
When we document we assert. We print to make real, to reify our being there.
When we do so with mindful intention to address our process, to open our work to others, to create beauty in words in space, to respect and acknowledge the strength of the page we now hold physical, a thing in our hand, we remind ourselves that, like Dorothy: *we had the power all along, my dears.*

THE PRINT! DOCUMENT SERIES
is a project of
the trouble with bartleby
in collaboration with
the operating system

THE FIELD OF INFINITE POSSIBILITIES